First Edition

Disclaimer: The recipes and nutritional information in this book are provided for informational purposes only. The author and publisher are not liable for any adverse reactions, effects, or consequences resulting from the use of any recipes or suggestions herein.

Cover design by Fetch & Read
Food photography by Fetch & Read

Printed in the United States of America,
by www.ingramspark.com.

ISBN 979-8-9944325-1-8

www.FetchandRead.com

Fetch more tail wagging recipes
and pup-approved treats, visit

www.FetchandRead.com

# Introduction

Welcome to the Paw-fect Birthday Cookbook!

This book was created with one goal in mind: to make your dog's special day as fun, delicious, and memorable as possible. Our furry friends give us unconditional love every single day, and what better way to celebrate them than with wholesome, homemade treats crafted just for them?

Inside these pages, you'll find easy-to-follow recipes made with simple, dog-safe ingredients. Everything from cakes and cookies to frozen goodies and pup-friendly drinks. Each recipe has been thoughtfully designed to be both tasty and nutritious, so you can spoil your pup without worry.

But this book isn't just about food. It's about creating joyful moments and lasting memories. Whether you're baking a birthday cake, whipping up everyday snacks, or throwing a full-on paw-ty, these recipes are meant to bring you closer to your best friend.

So grab your mixing bowl, gather your pup, and let's get cooking, because every dog deserves to feel extra special on their big day.

# Why Cook for Your Dog?

- **Healthier Ingredients:**
  You control what goes into every bite no hidden fillers or harmful additives.

- **Tailored to Your Pup:**
  Recipes can be adjusted for your dog's size, preferences, or dietary needs.

- **Bonding Time**
  Cooking for your dog is an act of love, and they'll feel it every time you share one of these homemade goodies.

- **Cost-Effective**
  Many recipes use affordable, everyday ingredients—saving money compared to premium store-bought treats.

- **Peace of Mind**
  You'll know exactly what your pup is eating, ensuring their snacks are both safe and delicious.

# INGREDIENTS & BENEFITS

| | |
|---|---|
| **Bananas** | Provide potassium, vitamin B6, and fiber, giving dogs a natural energy boost. |
| **Blueberries** | Packed with antioxidants and vitamin C, they support immunity and brain health. |
| **Watermelon (seedless)** | Hydrating and full of vitamins A and C, perfect as a refreshing treat. |
| **Strawberries** | Contain vitamin C and antioxidants, while naturally helping to whiten teeth. |
| **Carrots** | Rich in beta-carotene, they promote eye health and also clean teeth with their crunch. |
| **Sweet Potatoes** | High in fiber and vitamin B6, they provide long-lasting energy and aid digestion. |
| **Plain Potato** | Offer carbohydrates and potassium, but must be cooked plain to be safe. |
| **Pumpkin Purée** | A great source of fiber that regulates digestion and supports gut health. |
| **Mint Leaves** | Refresh breath naturally and provide antioxidants when used in small amounts. |
| **Ground Chicken** | A lean protein that's easy to digest and helps maintain muscle mass. |

# INGREDIENTS & BENEFITS

| | |
|---|---|
| **Ground Turkey** | Low in fat and high in protein, making it great for sensitive stomachs. |
| **Eggs** | Provide essential amino acids and fatty acids, boosting coat health and strong muscles. |
| **Whole Wheat Flour** | Adds fiber and nutrients, though best in moderation for sensitive dogs. |
| **Oat Flour / Rolled Oats** | Gentle on digestion, providing fiber and slow-release energy. |
| **Puffed Rice** | A light, low-calorie crunch that adds texture to treats. |
| **Baking Powder** | Used in tiny amounts to make treats fluffy, though too much can upset digestion. |
| **Ground Flax** | A source of omega-3s and fiber, promoting shiny coats and healthy digestion. |
| **Coconut Oil** | Improves skin and coat health, supports digestion, and provides quick energy. |
| **Olive Oil** | Contains healthy fats and antioxidants, supporting heart and coat wellness. |
| **Greek Yogurt (plain, unsweetened)** | Delivers probiotics for gut health along with protein and calcium. |

# INGREDIENTS & BENEFITS

| | |
|---|---|
| **Goat Milk** | Easier to digest than cow's milk and provides probiotics and fatty acids. |
| **Honey (only for dogs over 1 year)** | Provides antioxidants and natural energy in small amounts. |
| **Unsweetened Applesauce** | Acts as a natural sweetener and binder while adding vitamin C. |
| **Parsley** | Freshens breath and provides vitamins A, C, and K with anti-inflammatory benefits. |
| **Chickpeas** | Rich in protein and fiber, they aid digestion and muscle strength. |
| **Turmeric** | Acts as a natural anti-inflammatory that supports joint health. |
| **Carob Powder** | A dog-safe alternative to chocolate that adds antioxidants and fiber. |
| **Chicken Broth (low sodium)** | Boosts flavor and hydration while supplying essential minerals. |

# Disclaimer & Important Notes

Your dog's safety always comes first! While the recipes in this book use dog-safe ingredients, every pup is unique and may have different dietary needs or sensitivities.

##  Foods to Avoid for Dogs

- Chocolate & Cocoa
- Xylitol (artificial sweetener often found in peanut butter)
- Grapes & Raisins
- Onions & Garlic
- Macadamia Nuts
- Alcohol
- Caffeine
- Excessive Salt or Spices

##  Allergy Statement

Some dogs may have allergies or sensitivities to common ingredients like wheat, dairy, chicken, or eggs. Always introduce new foods slowly and watch for signs of an allergic reaction (such as itching, upset stomach, or changes in behavior).

If you're unsure about an ingredient or your dog has known health conditions, please consult your veterinarian before introducing new recipes.

# RECESPES

🍰 Cakes & Cupcakes
Peanut Butter & Banana Pupcake
Pumpkin Mini Cake
Mini Blueberry Bites

🍦Frozen Treats
Watermelon Pup Pops
Frozen Yogurt & Strawberry Bones
Peanut Butter & Banana Ice Cream

🍪 Cookies & Biscuits
Carrot Crunch Biscuits
Chicken & Sweet Potato Rounds
Apple Oat Birthday Cookies

🍿Party Snacks & Fun Foods
Paw-ty Popcorn
Mini Meatball Bites
Veggie Dippers with Dog-Friendly Hummus

🥄Frostings & Decorations
Yogurt & Peanut Butter Icing
Mashed Potato "Whipped Cream" Topping
Carob Ganache

🎉Extras
Doggie Birthday Punch
How to Make a DIY Birthday Hat or Pup Crown

# Peanut Butter & Banana Pupcakes

*Moist, flavorful, and pup-approved the perfect way to celebrate your dog's special day!*

## 🐾 Instructions

1. Preheat oven to 350ºF (175ºC). Line a muffin tin with silicone or paper liners.
2. Mash banana in medium mixing bowl until smooth.
3. Add peanut butter, **applesauce** and egg— whisk until combined.
4. Stir in flour and baking powder. Slowly add water until batter is thick but pourable.
5. Spoon batter evenly into muffin cups (about ¾ full).
6. Bake for 18-22 minutes, or until a toothpick inserted comes out
7. Cool completely on a wire rack before frosting.
8. Mix frosting ingredients together, then spread or pipe onto cooled pupcakes.

➡️ **Always serve in moderation as a treat, not a meal.**

## 🐾 Ingredients
### (Makes 6–8 Pupcakes):

- 1 ripe banana (mashed)
- ½ cup natural peanut butter (unsweetened, no xylitol)
- 1 cup whole wheat flour (or oat flour for gluten free option)
- 1 tsp baking powder
- ¼ cup unsweetened applesauce (or plain Greek yogurt)
- 1 egg  (or 1 tbsp ground flax + 3 tbsp water for egg-free)
- ⅓ cup water

## 🐾 Optional Frosting:

- ½ cup plain Greek yogurt
- 2 tbsp natural peanut butter
- 1 tsp honey (optional, only for dogs over 1 year old)

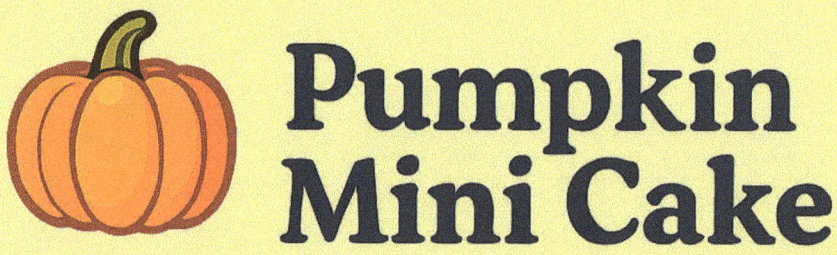

# Pumpkin Mini Cake

A quick, single-layer cake that's moist, healthy, and paw-fect for a doggie birthday celebration!

## 🐾 Ingredients
**(Makes 2-3 Mini Cakes)**

- ½ cup oat flour (or whole wheat flour)
- ½ tsp baking powder
- ¼ cup pumpkin purée (plain, unsweetened)
- 1 tbsp peanut butter (unsweetened, no xylitol)
- 1 tbsp coconut oil (melted)
- 1 egg

### Optional Frosting:
- ¼ cup plain Greek yogut
- 1 tsp peanut butter

## 🐾 Serving Size

Small dogs ➞ ½ mini cake

Medium dogs ➞ 1 mini cake

Large dogs ➞ up to 2 mini cakes

## 🍺 Instructions

1. Preheat oven to 350°F (175°C). Grease or line a muffin tin.
2. In a bowl, mix pumpkin, peanut butter, oil, and egg until smooth.
3. Stir in flour and baking powder until combined.
4. Divide batter evenly into muffin tin (2-3 wells).
5. Bake for 15-18 minutes, or until a toothpick comes out clean.

# Mini Blueberry Bites

A quick, fruity, no-fuss treat packed with antioxidants for your pup!

## Ingredients
### (Makes About 12 Bites)

- 1 cup oat flour
- ½ cup unsweetened applesauce
- ¼ cup fresh blueberries 🫐
- 1 tbsp coconut oil (melted)

## Instructions

1. Preheat oven to 350°F (175°C).
2. In a bowl, mix oat flour, applesauce, and coconut oil until a dough forms.
3. Gently fold in the blueberries
4. Roll into small bite-sized balls and place on a lined baking sheet.
5. Bake for 12–15 minutes, until firm.
6. Cool completely before serving.

   → *These are light, everyday treats — serve in moderation alongside meals.*

# WATERMELON PUP POPS

## 🐾 Ingredients:

- 2 cups seedless watermelon (cubed)
- 1/2 cup plain Greek yogurt (unsweetened, no added sugar)
- **1 tbsp honey** (optional, only for dogs over 1 year old)

**Optional Add-Ins:**

- 1/4 cup blueberries
- 2-3 mint leaves (for fresh breath, optional)

## 🐾 Instructions

1. Place watermelon cubes in a blender and puree until smooth.
2. Add Greek yogurt and honey, blending until fully combined.
3. Pour mixture into silicone molds, ice cube trays, or small paper cups.
4. (Optional) Drop a few blueberries or mint leaves into each mold for color and flavor.

## 🦴 Serving Size

Small dogs → 1-2 small pops
Medium dogs → 2-3 small pops
Large dogs → 3-4 **small pops**

→ Always supervise your dog while eating frozen treats to prevent gulping. Serve in moderation as a special snack.

# Frozen Yogurt & Strawberry Bones

*Cool, creamy, and fruity – a refreshing birthday treat that pups will love!*

## Ingredients

(Makes About 12 Bone-Shaped Treats)

- 1 cup plain Greek yogurt **(unsweetened, no added sugar)**
- ½ cup fresh strawberries, chopped
- 1 tbsp honey (optional, only for dogs over 1 year old)
- 1 tbsp water (if mixture is to thick for blending)

## Instructions

1. Wash and chop strawberries into small pieces.
2. Place strawberries, yogurt, and honey into a blender or food processor
3. Blend until smooth and creamy. Add a splash of water if needed
4. Pour mixture into bone-shaped silicone molds (or ice cube tray
5. Tap molds lightly on the counter to remove air bubbles.
6. Freeze for 4–5 hours, or until completely solid.
7. Pop out of molds and serve cold to your pup.

## Serving Size

Small dogs → 1-2 treats

Medium dogs → 2-3 treats

Large dogs → 3-4 treats

# Peanut Butter & Banana Ice Cream

A creamy, two-ingredient frozen treat that's ready in minutes!

## 🐾 Ingredients

**(Makes About 1½ Cups)**

- 2 ripe bananas, sliced and frozen
- 2 tbsp natural peanut butter (unsweetened, no xylitol)

## Instructions

1. Place frozen banana slices in a blender or food processor.

2. Blend until smooth and creamy.

3. Add peanut butter and blend again until fully combined.

## 🐾 Serving Size

Small dogs → 2 tbsp

Medium dogs → ¼ cup

Large dogs → ½ cup

*Always serve in moderation this is a treat, not a daily dessert.*

# Carrot Crunch Biscuits

Crunchy, veggie-packed biscuits your dog will love!

## Ingredients
### (Makes15 Biscuits)

- 1cup whole wheat flour
- ½ cup grated carrot
- ¼ cup unsweetened applesauce
- 1 egg

## Serving Size

- Small dogs →1 biscuit
- Medium dogs → 2 biscuits
- Large dogs → 3-4 biscuits

## 🏛 Instructions

1. Preheat oven to 350°F (175°C). Line a baking sheet with parchment paper.
2. In a bowl, combine grated carrot, applesauce, and egg. Mix well.
3. Stir in flour until dough forms.
4. Roll out dough on a lightly floured surface to about ¼-inch thick.
5. Cut into shapes using a bone or heart cookie cutter.
6. Place on baking sheet and bake for 15–18 minutes, until firm and lightly golden.
7. Cool completely before serving.

# Chicken & Sweet Potato Rounds

A simple two-ingredient recipe that bakes into chewy, savory rounds — perfect for birthdays or everyday spoiling!

## 🐾 Ingredients

**(Makes About 10-12**

- 1 medium sweet potato
- ½ cup cooked chicken breast, finely shredded

## Instructions

1. Preheat oven to 325°F (160°C). Line a baking sheet with parchment paper.
2. Peel and grate the sweet potato.
3. Mix grated sweet potato with shredded chicken until combined.
4. Scoop tablespoon-sized portions, roll into balls, and flatten slightly into rounds.
5. Place on baking sheet and bake for 25–30 minutes, flipping halfway, until firm and golden.
6. Cool completely before serving.

## 🐾 Serving Size

- Small dogs → 1 round
- Medium dogs → 2 rounds
- Large dogs → 3-4 rounds

→ *Store in the fridge for up to 4-5 days, or freeze for up to 1 month.*

# Apple Oat Birthday Cookies

A naturally sweet, crunchy cookie made with apple and oats – a healthy way to celebrate your pup's special day!

## 🐾 Ingredients
**(Makes About 15 Cookies)**

- 1 cup rolled oats (blended into oat flour)
- ½ cup unsweetened applesauce 🍎
- 1 tbsp peanut butter (unsweetened, no xylitol)
- 1 egg

## 🐾 Serving Size

- Small dogs → 1 cookie
- Medium dogs → 2 cookies
- Large dogs → 3-4 cookies
- → *These cookies are lightly sweet crunchy – perfect for birthdays or everyday snacks.*

## 🎛 Instructions

1. Preheat oven to 350°F (175°C). Line a baking sheet with parchment paper.
2. Blend oats into a fine flour if needed.
3. In a bowl, mix oat flour, applesauce, peanut butter, and egg into a dough.
4. Roll dough into small balls and flatten slightly with your hand or a fork.
5. Place on baking sheet and bake for 12–15 minutes, until firm and lightly golden.
6. Cool completely before serving.

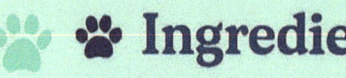

# Paw-ty Popcorn

## (Puffed Rice with Peanut Butter Drizzle)

A crunchy, birthday-ready treat with a yummy peanut butter drizzle your pup will love!

## Ingredients
### (Makes About 2 Cups)

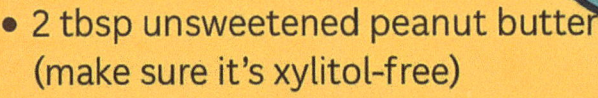

- 2 cups plain puffed rice (unsweetened, no added sugar)
- 2 tbsp unsweetened peanut butter (make sure it's xylitol-free)
- 1 tsp coconut oil (melted)

## Instructions

1. Place puffed rice in a large mixing bowl.
2. In a small microwave-safe dish, gently warm the peanut butter and coconut oil together for about 20–30 seconds until smooth and pourable.
3. Drizzle the peanut butter mixture over the puffed rice.
4. Stir well to coat evenly.
5. Spread onto a parchment-lined tray and let cool for 15 minutes so the drizzle firms up.

## Serving Size

- Small dogs → 1–2 tbsp
- Medium dogs → ¼ cup
- Large dogs → ½ cup

# Mini Meatball Bites

Tender, bite-sized meatballs made with lean protein and wholesome ingredients—a savory treat your pup will love!

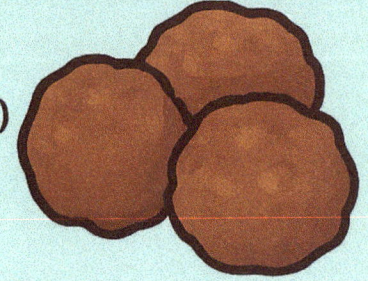

## Ingredients
**(Makes About 12 Meatballs)**

- ½ lb ground chicken or turkey (lean)
- ¼ cup oat flour (or ground rolled oats)
- 1 egg
- 2 tbsp grated carrot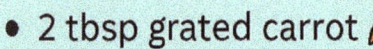
- 1 tbsp parsley (optional, for fresh breath)

## Serving Size

- Small dogs → 1 meatball
- Medium dogs → 2 meatballs
- Large dogs → 3–4 meatballs

→ *Store in an airtight container in the fridge for up to 3 days, or freeze for longer storage.*

##  Instructions

1. Preheat oven to 350°F (175°C). Line a baking sheet with parchment paper.

2. In a bowl, combine ground meat, oat flour, egg, carrot, and parsley. Mix well.

3. Roll mixture into small, bite-sized meatballs (about 1 inch).

4. Place on baking sheet and bake for 15–18 min.

5. Allow to cool before servin

# Veggie Dippers with Dog-Friendly Hummus

A crunchy, fresh snack paired with a smooth, dog-safe hummus — paw-fect for paw-ty platters!

## Ingredients

**(Makes About 1 Cup Hummus + Veggie Sticks)**

- 1 cup cooked chickpeas (rinsed and drained)
- 2 tbsp plain Greek yogurt (unsweetened)
- 1 tbsp olive oil
- 1–2 tbsp water (to thin, as needed)
- ½ tsp turmeric (optional, for anti-inflammatory benefits)

## For the Dippers:

- Carrot sticks
- Cucumber sticks
- Zucchini sticks

Store hummus in the fridge for up to 3 days. Serve veggies fresh and crunchy.

## Instructions

1. In a blender or food processor, combine chickpeas, yogurt, olive oil, and turmeric. Blend until smooth, adding water a little at a time for a creamy consistency.
2. Slice veggies into sticks for dipping.
3. Serve hummus in a small bowl with veggie sticks around it.

# Yogurt & Peanut Butter Icing

A simple and tasty icing for pupcakes, cookies, or any dog treat.

## Ingredients

- ¼ cup plain Greek yogurt (unsweetened, no artificial sweeteners)
- 2 tbsp unsweetened peanut butter (xylitol-free)
- 1 tsp honey (optional, for dogs over 1 year old)

## Instructions

1. In a small bowl, stir together the yogurt and peanut butter until smooth.
2. Add honey if using, and mix well.
3. Use immediately to frost pupcakes, biscuits, or mini cakes.

### 🐕 Tips

- If the mixture is too thick, add ½–1 tsp of water until it spreads easily.
- Store leftover icing in the fridge for up to 3 days.
- For a firmer texture, refrigerate icing for 15–20 minutes before piping or spreading.

# Mashed Potato 'Whipped Cream" Topping

A decorative, creamy topping for cakes, with a mashed potato base.

## Ingredients
### (Makes About 2 Cups)

- 1 medium potato (peeled and chopped)
- 2 tbsp plain Greek yogurt (unsweetened)
- 1 tbsp low-sodium chicken broth (optional, for flavor)

### 🐾 Tips

- For piping, let the mash cool completely and place in a piping bag with a star tip.
- Store leftovers in the fridge for up to 3 days.
- Make sure the potatoes are plain — no butter, milk, salt, or seasoning.

## Instructions

1. Peel and chop the potato, then boil until fork-tender (about 10–12 minutes).
2. Drain and mash the potato until smooth.
3. Stir in Greek yogurt (and chicken broth if using) until fluffy and creamy.
4. Chill slightly, then spoon or pipe onto pupcakes or mini cakes like whipped cream.

# Carob Ganache

A creamy, decadent "chocolate-style" topping made with carob, perfect for drizzling or frosting pupcakes, cakes, or cookies.

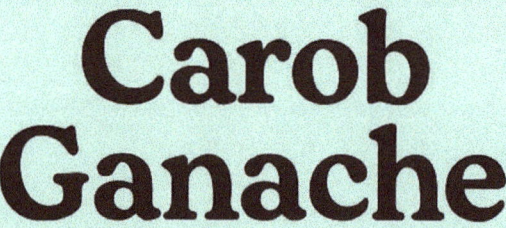

## Ingredients
### (Makes About ½ Cup)

- ¼ cup carob powder
- 2 tbsp coconut oil (melted)
- 2 tbsp plain Greek yogurt (unsweetened)
- 1-2 tsp honey (optional, only for dogs over 1 year old)

## Instructions

1. In a small bowl, whisk together the carob powder and melted coconut oil until smooth.
2. Stir in Greek yogurt until creamy.
3. Add honey (if using) and mix well.
4. Use immediately to drizzle over cakes or spread as frosting.

## 🐾 Tips

- If too thick, add 1 tsp of warm water to thin.
- Store leftovers in the fridge for up to 3 days.

# BIRTHDAY EXTRAS

# Doggie Birthday Punch

A cool, festive drink made with creamy goat's milk, sweet blueberries, and a touch of honey – perfect for celebrating your pup's big day!

## Ingredients
### (Makes About 2 Cups)

- 1 ½ cups plain goat's milk
- ¼ cup fresh blueberries
- 1 tsp honey (optional, only for dogs over 1 year old)
- A few ice cubes ❄️

## Serving Size

- Small dogs → ¼ cup
- Medium dogs → ½ cup
- Large dogs → 1 cup

## Instructions

1. Add goat's milk, blueberries, and honey to a blender.
2. Blend until smooth and slightly frothy.
3. Pour into a dog-safe bowl or cup.
4. Add a couple of ice cubes for extra chill.
5. Serve fresh as a special birthday toast!

→ Always serve in moderation. Store leftovers in the fridge for up to 2 days.

# DIY Birthday Hat or Pup Crown

## Materials

- Colorful cardstock or construction paper
- Non-toxic markers, stickers, or glitter for decorating
- Elastic string or soft ribbon
- Scissors ✂️
- Tape or a stapler

## Instructions

1. Choose your style → Cut the cardstock into either a tall cone (hat) or a wide band (crown).
2. Decorate → Use markers, stickers, or glitter to make it paw-some. You can even add your pup's name!
3. Fit to size → Gently measure around your pup's head and trim the base of the hat/crown to fit comfortably.
4. Attach strap → Tape or staple elastic/ribbon to the sides. Make sure it's snug but not tight.
5. Crown your pup → Place the hat/crown on their head and get ready for adorable birthday photos!

💡 Tip: Keep it lightweight and comfy so your pup enjoys wearing it — even if only for pictures!

# Thank You

From the bottom of my heart, thank you for joining me on this journey and for choosing to share these recipes with your pup.

Every recipe in this book was created with love, with the hope that each tail wag, happy bark, and eager lick reminds you of the joy our dogs bring into our lives. They are more than pets, they are family.

By taking the time to make healthy, homemade treats, you're giving your dog more than just food:

You're giving them wellness, by nourishing their bodies with safe, wholesome ingredients.

You're giving them happiness, because good food lifts their mood, brightens their spirit, and fills their day with joy.

Most importantly, you're giving them love. The kind they'll return endlessly, in every cuddle, every wag, and every look that says, "You are my favorite person."

This book isn't just about recipes. It's about deepening the bond between you and your best friend. Healthy treats and meals are one of the many ways to say, "I love you." And dogs, with their big hearts and loyal souls, will love you back a thousand times more for it.

So here's to you, your pup, and the countless moments of happiness these recipes will bring. May every bite remind you of the incredible gift we have in our dogs—unconditional love.

www.ingramcontent.com/pod-product-compliance
Lightning Source LLC
Chambersburg PA
CBHW051600120626
46551CB00013B/1605